This informational booklet is intended
to provide a generic, non-exhaustive
overview of a particular standards-
related topic. This publication does
not itself alter or determine compliance responsibilities, which are set
forth in OSHA standards themselves
and the *Occupational Safety and
Health Act*. Moreover, because
interpretations and enforcement policy
may change over time, for additional
guidance on OSHA compliance
requirements, the reader should
consult current administrative interpretations and decisions by the Occupational Safety and Health Review
Commission and the courts.

Material contained in this publication
is in the public domain and may be
reproduced, fully or partially, without
permission of the Federal Government.
Source credit is requested by not
required.

This information will be made
available to sensory impaired
individuals upon request.
Voice phone: (202) 219-8615;
Telecommunications Device for the
Deaf (TDD) referral phone:
1-800-326-2577.

# Chemical Hazard Communication

U.S. Department of Labor
Alexis M. Herman, Secretary

Occupational Safety and Health Administration
Charles N. Jeffress, Assistant Secretary

OSHA 3084
1998 (Revised)

# Contents

Page

Under the provisions of the Hazard Communication Standard, employers are responsible for informing employees of the hazards and the identities of workplace chemicals to which they are exposed.

About 32 million workers work with and are potentially exposed to one or more chemical hazards. There are an estimated 650,000 existing chemical products, and hundreds of new ones being introduced annually. This poses a serious problem for exposed workers and their employers.

Chemical exposure may cause or contribute to many serious health effects such as heart ailments, central nervous system, kidney and lung damage, sterility, cancer, burns, and rashes. Some chemicals may also be safety hazards and have the potential to cause fires and explosions and other serious accidents.

Because of the seriousness of these safety and health problems, and because many employers and employees know little or nothing about them, the Occupational Safety and Health Administration (OSHA) issued the Hazard Communication Standard. The basic goal of the standard is to be sure employers and employees know about work hazards and how to protect themselves; this should help to reduce the incidence of chemical source illness and injuries.

The Hazard Communication Standard establishes uniform requirements to make sure that the hazards of all chemicals imported into, produced, or used in U.S. workplaces are evaluated, and that this hazard information is transmitted to affected employers and exposed employees.

Employers and employees covered by an OSHA-approved state safety and health plan should check with their state agency, which may be enforcing standards and other procedures "at least as effective as," but not always identical to, federal requirements. See also pages 13 and 18 of this publication for more information on state plans.

Basically, the hazard communication standard is different from other OSHA health rules because it covers all hazardous chemicals. The rule also incorporates a "downstream flow of information," which means that producers of chemicals have the primary responsibility for generating and disseminating information, whereas users of chemicals must obtain the information and transmit it to their own employees. In general, it works like this:

| | |
|---|---|
| **Chemical Manufacturers/ Importers** | • Determine the hazards of each product. |
| **Chemical Manufacturers/ Importers/ Distributors** | • Communicate the hazard information and associated protective measures downstream to customers through labels and MSDSs. |
| **Employers** | • Identify and list hazardous chemicals in their workplaces.<br>• Obtain MSDSs and labels for each hazardous chemical, if not provided by the manufacturer, importer, or distributor.<br>• Develop and implement a written hazard communication program, including labels, MSDSs, and employee training, on the list of chemicals, MSDSs and label information.<br>• Communicate hazard information to their employees through labels, MSDSs, and formal training programs. |

OSHA's standard *(Title 29, Code of Federal Regulations, Part 1910.1200, 1915.99, 1917.28, 1918.90, and 1926.59 )* applies to general industry, shipyard, marine terminals, longshoring, and construction employment and covers chemical manufacturers, importers, employers, and employees exposed to chemical hazards.

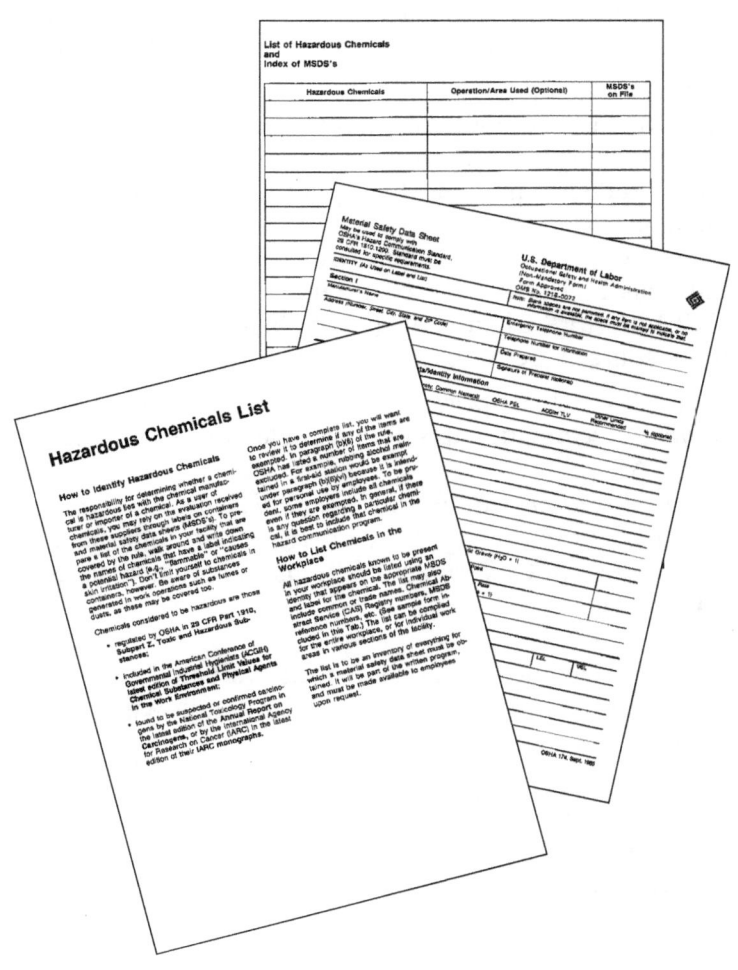

The quality of the hazard communication program depends on the adequacy and accuracy of the assessment of hazards in the workplace. Chemical manufacturers and importers are required to review available scientific evidence concerning the hazards of the chemicals they produce or import, and to report the information they find to their employees and to employers who distribute or use their products. Downstream employers can rely on the evaluations performed by the chemical manufacturers or importers to establish the hazards of the chemicals they use.

The chemical manufacturers, importers, and any employers who choose to evaluate hazards are responsible for the quality of the hazard determinations they perform. Each chemical must be evaluated for its potential to cause adverse health effects and its potential to pose physical hazards such as flammability. (Definitions of hazards covered are included in the standard, see 1910.1200(c).) Chemicals that are listed in one of the following sources are to be considered hazardous in all cases:

- *29 CFR 1910, Subpart Z, Toxic and Hazardous Substances*, Occupational Safety and Health Administration (OSHA), and
- *Threshold Limit Values for Chemical Substances and Physical Agents in the Work Environment*, American Conference of Governmental Industrial Hygienists (ACGIH).

In addition, chemicals that have been evaluated and found to be a suspect or confirmed carcinogen in the following sources must be reported as such:

- National Toxicology Program (NTP), *Annual Report on Carcinogens,*
- International Agency for Research on Cancer (IARC), *Monographs*, and
- Regulated by OSHA as a carcinogen.

A written hazard communication program ensures that all employers receive the information they need to inform and train their employees properly and to design and put in place employee protection programs. It also provides necessary hazard information to employees, so they can participate in, and support, the protective measures in place at their workplaces.

Employers therefore must develop, implement, and maintain at the workplace a written, comprehensive hazard communication program that includes provisions for container labeling, collection and availability of material safety data sheets, and an employee training program. It also must contain a list of the hazardous chemicals, the means the employer will use to inform employees of the hazards of non-routine tasks (for example, the cleaning of reactor vessels), and the hazards associated with chemicals in unlabeled pipes. If the workplace has multiple employers onsite (for example, a construction site), the rule requires these employers to ensure that information regarding hazards and protective measures be made available to the other employers onsite, where appropriate. In addition, all covered employers must have a written hazard communication program to get hazard information to their employees through labels on containers, MSDSs, and training.

The written program does not have to be lengthy or complicated, and some employers may be able to rely on existing hazard communication programs to comply with the above requirements. The written program must be available to employees, their designated representatives, the Assistant Secretary of Labor for Occupational Safety and Health, and the Director of the National Institute for Occupational Safety and Health (NIOSH).

(Sample programs are available in the Compliance Directive CPL 2-2.38 D, Appendix E. Also, see *Hazard Communication—A Compliance Kit* (OSHA 3104) (a reference guide to step- by-step requirements for compliance with the OSHA standard.) The kit can be obtained from the Government Printing Office.
(See **OSHA Related Publications** for ordering information.)

Chemical manufacturers and importers must convey the hazard information they learn from their evaluations to downstream employers by means of labels on containers and material safety data sheets (MSDSs).

Also, chemical manufacturers, importers, and distributors must be sure that containers of hazardous chemicals leaving the workplace are labeled, tagged, or marked with the identity of the chemical, appropriate hazard warnings, and the name and address of the manufacturer or other responsible party.

In the workplace, each container must be labeled, tagged, or marked with the identity of hazardous chemicals contained therein, and must show hazard warnings appropriate for employee protection. The hazard warning can be any type of message, words, pictures, or symbols that provide at least general information regarding the hazards of the chemical(s) in the container and the targeted organs affected, if applicable. Labels must be legible, in English (plus other languages, if desired), and prominently displayed.

Exemptions to the requirement for in-plant individual container labels are as follows:

- Employers can post signs or placards that convey the hazard information if there are a number of stationary containers within a work area that have similar contents and hazards.
- Employers can substitute various types of standard operating procedures, process sheets, batch tickets, blend tickets, and similar written materials for container labels on stationary process equipment if they contain the same information and the written materials are readily accessible to employees in the work area.
- Employers are not required to label portable containers into which hazardous chemicals are transferred from labeled containers and that are intended only for the immediate use of the employee who makes the transfer.
- Employers are not required to label pipes or piping systems.

The MSDS is a detailed information bulletin prepared by the manufacturer or importer of a chemical that describes the physical and chemical properties, physical and health hazards, routes of exposure, precautions for safe handling and use, emergency and first-aid procedures, and control measures.

Chemical manufacturers and importers must develop an MSDS for each hazardous chemical they produce or import, and must provide the MSDS automatically at the time of the initial shipment of a hazardous chemical to a downstream distributor or user. Distributors also must ensure that downstream employers are similarly provided an MSDS.

Each MSDS must be in English and include information regarding the specific chemical identity of the hazardous chemical(s) involved and the common names. In addition, information must be provided on the physical and chemical characteristics of the hazardous chemical; known acute and chronic health effects and related health information; exposure limits; whether the chemical is considered to be a carcinogen by NTP, IARC, or OSHA; precautionary measures; emergency and first-aid procedures; and the identification (name, address, and telephone number) of the organization responsible for preparing the sheet.

Copies of the MSDS for hazardous chemicals in a given worksite are to be readily accessible to employees in that area. As a source of detailed information on hazards, they must be readily available to workers during each workshift. MSDSs have no prescribed format. ANSI standard no. Z400.1—*Material Safety Data Sheet Preparation*—may be used. The non-mandatory MSDS form (OSHA 174) also may be used as a guide and a copy can be obtained from OSHA field offices.

Employers must prepare a list of all hazardous chemicals in the workplace. When the list is complete, it should be checked against the collected MSDSs that the employer has been sent.

If there are hazardous chemicals used for which no MSDS has been received, the employer must contact the supplier, manufacturer, or importer to obtain the missing MSDS. A record of the contact must be maintained.

Employers must establish a training and information program for employees who are exposed to hazardous chemicals in their work area at the time of initial assignment and whenever a new hazard is introduced into their work area.

At a minimum, the discussion topics must include the following:

- The hazard communication standard and its requirements.
- The components of the hazard communication program in the employees' workplaces.
- Operations in work areas where hazardous chemicals are present.
- Where the employer will keep the written hazard evaluation procedures, communications program, lists of hazardous chemicals, and the required MSDS forms.

The employee training plan must consist of the following elements:

- How the hazard communication program is implemented in that workplace, how to read and interpret information on labels and the MSDS, and how employees can obtain and use the available hazard information.
- The hazards of the chemicals in the work area. (The hazards may be discussed by individual chemical or by hazard categories such as flammability.)
- Measures employees can take to protect themselves from the hazards.
- Specific procedures put into effect by the employer to provide protection such as engineering controls, work practices, and the use of personal protective equipment (PPE).
- Methods and observations—such as visual appearance or smell—workers can use to detect the presence of a hazardous chemical to which they may be exposed.

A "trade secret" is something that gives an employer an opportunity to obtain an advantage over competitors who do not know about the trade secret or who do not use it. For example, a trade secret may be a confidential device, pattern, information, or chemical make-up. Chemical industry trade secrets are generally formulas, process data, or a "specific chemical identity." The latter is the type of trade secret information referred to in the Hazard Communication Standard. The term includes the chemical name, the Chemical Abstracts Services (CAS) Registry Number, or any other specific information that reveals the precise designation. It does not extend to PELs or TLVs. If the hazardous chemical or a component thereof has a PEL or TLV, this must be reflected on the MSDS.

The standard strikes a balance between the need to protect exposed employees and the employer's need to maintain the confidentiality of a bona fide trade secret. This is achieved by providing for limited disclosure to health professionals who are furnishing medical or other occupational health services to exposed employees, employees and their designated representatives, under specified conditions of need and confidentiality.

The chemical manufacturer, importer, or employer must immediately disclose the specific chemical identity of a hazardous chemical to a treating physician or nurse when the information is needed for proper emergency or first-aid treatment. As soon as circumstances permit, the chemical manufacturer, importer, or employer may obtain a written statement of need and a confidentiality agreement.

Under the contingency described here, the treating physician or nurse has the ultimate responsibility for determining that a medical emergency exists. At the time of the emergency, the professional judgment of the physician or nurse regarding the situation must form the basis for triggering the immediate disclosure requirement. Because the chemical manufacturer, importer, or employer can demand a written statement of need and a confidentiality agreement to be completed after the emergency is abated, further disclosure of the trade secret can be effectively controlled.

In non-emergency situations, chemical manufacturers, importers, or employers must disclose the withheld specific chemical identity to health professionals providing medical or other occupational health services to exposed employees, and to employees and their designated representatives, if certain conditions are met. In this context, "health professionals" include physicians, occupational health nurses, industrial hygienists, toxicologists, or epidemiologists.

The request for information must be in writing and must describe with reasonable detail the medical or occupational health need for the information. The request will be considered if the information will be used for one or more of the following activities:

- To assess the hazards of the chemicals to which employees will be exposed.
- To conduct or assess sampling of the workplace atmosphere to determine employee exposure levels.
- To conduct pre-assignment or periodic medical surveillance of exposed employees.
- To provide medical treatment to exposed employees.
- To select or assess appropriate personal protective equipment for exposed employees.
- To design or assess engineering controls or other protective measures for exposed employees.
- To conduct studies to determine the health effects of exposure.

The health professional, employee, or designated representative must also specify why alternative information is insufficient. The request for information must explain in detail why disclosure of the specific chemical identity is essential, and include the procedures to be used to protect the confidentiality of the information. It must include an agreement not to use the information for any purpose other than the health need stated or to release it under any circumstances, except to OSHA.

The standard further describes in detail the steps that will be followed in the event that an employer decides not to disclose the specific chemical identity requested by the health professional, employee, or designated representative. (See 1910.1200( i)(7).)

OSHA offers a variety of programs and initiatives to help employers comply with the agency's standards or guidelines. The following is a brief summary of some of these efforts.

### Safety and Health Program Management Guidelines

Effective management of worker safety and health protection is a decisive factor in reducing the extent and severity of work-related injuries and illnesses and their related costs. To assist employers and employees in developing effective safety and health programs, OSHA published recommended *Safety and Health Program Management Guidelines (Federal Register 54 (18): 3908-3916, January 26, 1989)*. These voluntary guidelines apply to all places of employment covered by OSHA.

The guidelines identify four general elements that are critical to the development of a successful safety and health management program:

- Management commitment and employee involvement,
- Worksite analysis,
- Hazard prevention and control, and
- Safety and health training.

The guidelines recommend specific action, under each of these general elements to achieve an effective safety and health program. A single free copy of the guidelines can be obtained from the U.S. Department of Labor, OSHA Publications, P.O. Box 37535, Washington, DC 20013-7535, by sending a self-addressed mail label with your request.

(Available on the World Wide Web under Federal Register, http://www.osha.gov/).

## State Programs

The *Occupational Safety and Health Act of 1970* encourages states to develop and operate their own job safety and health plans. States with plans approved under section 18(b) of the Act must adopt standards and enforce requirements that are at least as effective as federal requirements. There are currently 25 state plan states and territories: 23 of these states administer plans covering both private and public (state and local government) employees; the other 2 states, Connecticut and New York, cover public employees only.

Plan states must adopt standards comparable to federal requirements within 6 months of a federal standard's promulgation. Until a state standard is promulgated, OSHA will provide interim enforcement assistance, as appropriate, in these states. A listing of approved state plans appears at the end of this publication.

## Consultation Services

Consultation assistance is available on request to employers who want help in establishing and maintaining a safe and healthful workplace. Largely funded by OSHA, the service is provided at no cost to the employer. Primarily developed for smaller employers with more hazardous operations, the consultation service is delivered by state government agencies or universities employing professional safety and health consultants. Comprehensive assistance includes an appraisal of all mechanical systems, physical work practices and occupational safety and health hazards of the workplace, and all aspects of the employer's present job safety and health program.

In addition, the service offers assistance to employers in developing and implementing an effective safety and health program. No penalties are proposed or citations issued for any safety or health problems identified by the consultant. The service is confidential.

For more information concerning consultation assistance, see the list of consultation projects at the end of this publication.

## Voluntary Protection Programs (VPPs)

Voluntary Protection Programs and onsite consultation services, when coupled with an effective enforcement program, expand worker protection to help meet the goals of the OSH Act. The three VPPs—Star, Merit, and Demonstration—are designed to recognize outstanding achievement by companies that have successfully incorporated comprehensive safety and health programs into their total management system. The VPPs motivate others to achieve excellent safety and health results in the same outstanding way as they establish a cooperative relationship among employers, employees, and OSHA.

For additional information on VPPs and how to apply, contact the OSHA area or regional offices listed at the end of this publication.

## Training and Education

OSHA's area offices offer a variety of information services, such as publications, audiovisual aids, technical advice, and speakers for special engagements. OSHA's Training Institute in Des Plaines, IL, provides basic and advanced courses in safety and health for federal and state compliance officers, state consultants, federal agency personnel, and private sector employers, employees, and their representatives.

The OSHA Training Institute also has established OSHA Training Institute Education Centers to address the increased demand for its courses from the private sector and from other federal agencies. These centers are nonprofit colleges, universities, and other organizations that have been selected after a competition for participation in the program. They are located in various parts of the U.S.

OSHA also provides funds to nonprofit organizations, through grants, to conduct workplace training and education in subjects where OSHA believes there is a lack of workplace training. Grants are awarded annually and grant recipients are expected to contribute 20 percent of the total grant cost.

For more information on grants, training and education, contact the OSHA Training Institute, Office of Training and Education, 1555 Times Drive, Des Plaines, IL 60018, (847) 297-4810.

For further information on any OSHA program, contact your nearest OSHA area or regional office listed at the end of this publication.

## Electronic Information

Internet—OSHA standards, interpretations, directives, and additional information are now on the World Wide Web at http://www.osha.gov.

CD-ROM—A wide variety of OSHA materials—including standards, interpretations, directives, and more—can be purchased on CD-ROM from the U.S. Government Printing Office, Superintendent of Documents.

To order, write to the Superintendent of Documents, P.O. Box 371954, Pittsburgh, PA 15250-7954. Specify *OSHA Regulations, Documents and Technical Information on* CD ROM, *(ORDT)*, S/N 729-1300000-5. The price is $38 per year ($47.50 foreign); a single copy is $15.00 ($18.75 foreign). The phone number is (202) 512-1800.

## Emergencies

For life-threatening situations, call (800) 321-OSHA. Complaints will go immediately to the nearest OSHA area or state office for help.

For further information on any OSHA program, contact your nearest OSHA area or regional office listed at the end of this publication.

Yes. OSHA has developed a variety of materials and publications to help employers and employees develop and implement effective hazard communication programs. Lists of products, services, and other resources are as follows:

## OSHA Related Publications

A single free copy of the following publications can be obtained from the U.S. Department of Labor, OSHA Publications Office, P.O. Box 37535, Washington, DC 20013-7535, (202) 219-4677, (202) 219-9266 (fax), or from the nearest OSHA regional or area office listed at the end of this publication. Send a self-addressed mailing label with your request.

These and other products can be ordered or downloaded from OSHA's Web Site at http://www.osha.gov.

*All About OSHA*—OSHA 2056

*Consultation Services for the Employer*—OSHA 3047

*Employee Workplace Rights*—OSHA 3021

*How to Prepare for Workplace Emergencies*—OSHA 3088

*OSHA Inspections*—OSHA 2098

*Personal Protective Equipment*—OSHA 3077

*Respiratory Protection*—OSHA 3079

*Hazard Communication; Final Rule. Federal Register* 59(27): 6126-6184, February 9, 1994.

The following publications are available from the Superintendent of Documents, U.S. Government Printing Office, Washington, DC 20402, phone (202) 512-1800, fax (202) 512-2250. Include GPO Order No. and make checks payable to Superintendent of Documents.

*Hazard Communication—A Compliance Kit—*
OSHA 3104 (A reference guide to step-by-step requirements for compliance with the OSHA standard.)
Order No. 029-016-00147-6; cost $18.00 domestic; $22.50 foreign.

**Hazard Communication Guidelines for Compliance—**
OSHA 3111
Order No. 029-016-00163-8; cost $1.50.

*Job Hazard Analysis*—OSHA 3071
Order No. 029-016-00142-5; cost $1.00.

**Training Requirements in OSHA Standards and Training Guidelines**—OSHA 2254
Order No. 029-016-00160-3; cost $6.00.

## National Technical Information Services Related Materials

The following materials are available from the National Technical Information Services, 5285 Port Royal Road, Springfield, VA 22161, phone (703) 605-6000. Web site is http://www.ntis.gov.

*Eye Injuries and Eye Protection Equipment—*
AVA 14624, SSOO, $99.

*Safety and Health Factors for Working with Formalde—hyde* - AVA 17500, SSOO, $99.

*Safety and Health Factors with Temperature Stress—*
AVA 14626, SSOO, $99.

*Safety and Health Factors for Working with Silica—*
AVA 20000, SSOO, $90.

*Safety and Health Requirements for Working with Carbon Monoxide*—AVA 19005, SSOO, $139.

*Safety and Health Factors in Welding and Cutting—*
AVA 18463,VNB1, $99.

**Commissioner**
Alaska Department of Labor
1111 West 8th Street
Room 306
Juneau, AK 99801
(907) 465-2700

**Director**
Industrial Commission
 of Arizona
800 W. Washington
Phoenix, AZ 85007
(602) 542-5795

**Director**
California Department
 of Industrial Relations
45 Fremont Street
San Francisco, CA 94105
(415) 972-8835

**Commissioner**
Connecticut Department
 of Labor
200 Folly Brook Boulevard
Wethersfield, CT 06109
(860) 566-5123

**Director**
Hawaii Department of Labor
 and Industrial Relations
830 Punchbowl Street
Honolulu, HI 96813
(808) 586-8844

**Commissioner**
Indiana Department of Labor
State Office Building
402 West Washington Street
Room W195
Indianapolis, IN 46204
(317) 232-2378

**Commissioner**
Iowa Division of Labor
 Services
1000 E. Grand Avenue
Des Moines, IA 50319
(515) 281-3447

**Secretary**
Kentucky Labor Cabinet
1047 U.S. Highway, 127
South, STE 2
Frankfort, KY 40601
(502) 564-3070

**Commissioner**
Maryland Division of Labor
 and Industry
Department of Labor
 Licensing and Regulation
1100 N. Eutaw Street,
Room 613
Baltimore, MD 21201-2206
(410) 767-2215

**Director**
Michigan Department
  of Consumer
  and Industry Services
4th Floor, Law Building
P.O. Box 30004
Lansing, MI 48909
(517) 373-7230

**Commissioner**
Minnesota Department
  of Labor and Industry
443 Lafayette Road
St. Paul, MN 55155
(612) 296-2342

**Administrator**
Nevada Division of Industrial
  Relations
400 West King Street
Carson City, NV 89710
(702) 687-3032

**Secretary**
New Mexico Environment
  Department
1190 St. Francis Drive
P.O. Box 26110
Santa Fe, NM 87502
(505) 827-2850

**Commissioner**
New York Department
  of Labor
W. Averell Harriman State
Office
  Building - 12, Room 500
Albany, NY 12240
(518) 457-2741

**Commissioner**
North Carolina Department
  of Labor
319 Chapanoke Road
Raleigh, NC 27603
(919) 662-4585

**Administrator**
Department of Consumer
  & Business Services
Occupational Safety
  and Health Division
  (OR-OSHA)
350 Winter Street, NE,
Room 430
Salem, OR 97310-0220
(503) 378-3272

**Secretary**
Puerto Rico Department
  of Labor and Human
    Resources
Prudencio Rivera Martinez
Building
505 Munoz Rivera Avenue
Hato Rey, PR 00918
(809) 754-2119

**Director**
South Carolina Department
 of Labor
Licensing and Regulation
Koger Office Park, Kingstree
 Building
110 Centerview Drive
P.O. Box 11329
Columbia, SC 29210
(803) 896-4300

**Commissioner**
Tennessee Department
 of Labor
710 James Robertson
 Parkway
Nashville, TN 37243-0659
(615) 741-2582

**Commissioner**
Industrial Commission
 of Utah
160 East 300 South, 3rd Floor
P.O. Box 146650
Salt Lake City, UT 84114-
 6650
(801) 530-6898

**Commissioner**
Vermont Department
 of Labor and Industry
National Life Building -
Drawer 20
120 State Street
Montpelier, VT 05620-3401
(802) 828-2288

**Commissioner**
Virginia Department of Labor
 and Industry
Powers-Taylor Building
13 South 13th Street
Richmond, VA 23219
(804) 786-2377

**Commissioner**
Virgin Islands Department
 of Labor
2131 Hospital Street, Box 890
Christiansted
St. Croix, VI 00820-4666
(809) 773-1994

**Director**
Washington Department
 of Labor and Industries
General Administrative
 Building
P.O. Box 44001
Olympia, WA 98504-4001
(360) 902-4200

**Administrator**
Worker's Safety and
 Compensation Division (WSC)
Wyoming Department
 of Employment
Herschler Building,
 2nd Floor East
122 West 25th Street
Cheyenne, WY 82002
(307) 777-7786

| State | Telephone |
|---|---|
| Alabama | (205) 348-7136 |
| Alaska | (907) 269-4957 |
| Arizona | (602) 542-5795 |
| Arkansas | (501) 682-4522 |
| California | (415) 972-8515 |
| Colorado | (970) 491-6151 |
| Connecticut | (860) 566-4550 |
| Delaware | (302) 761-8219 |
| District of Columbia | (202) 576-6339 |
| Florida | (904) 488-3044 |
| Georgia | (404) 894-2643 |
| Guam | 011 (671) 475-0136 |
| Hawaii | (808) 586-9100 |
| Idaho | (208) 385-3283 |
| Illinois | (312) 814-2337 |
| Indiana | (317) 232-2688 |
| Iowa | (515) 965-7162 |
| Kansas | (913) 296-7476 |
| Kentucky | (502) 564-6895 |
| Louisiana | (504) 342-9601 |
| Maine | (207) 624-6460 |
| Maryland | (410) 880-4970 |
| Massachusetts | (617) 727-3982 |
| Michigan | (517) 322-1817 (H) |
|  | (517) 322-1809 (S) |
| Minnesota | (612) 297-2393 |
| Mississippi | (601) 987-3981 |
| Missouri | (573) 751-3403 |
| Montana | (406) 444-6418 |
| Nebraska | (402) 471-4717 |
| Nevada | (702) 486-5016 |
| New Hampshire | (603) 271-2024 |
| New Jersey | (609) 292-2424 |
| New Mexico | (505) 827-4230 |
| New York | (518) 457-2481 |
| North Carolina | (919) 662-4644 |

North Dakota ....................................................... (701) 328-5188
Ohio .................................................................... (614) 644-2246
Oklahoma ........................................................... (405) 528-1500
Oregon ............................................................... (503) 378-3272
Pennsylvania ...................................................... (412) 357-2561
Puerto Rico ........................................................ (787) 754-2188
Rhode Island ...................................................... (401) 277-2438
South Carolina ................................................... (803) 896-4300
South Dakota ..................................................... (605) 688-4101
Tennessee ........................................................... (615) 741-7036
Texas ................................................................. (512) 440-3809
Utah ................................................................... (801) 530-7606
Vermont ............................................................. (802) 828-2765
Virginia .............................................................. (804) 786-6359
Virgin Islands..................................................... (809) 772-1315
Washington ........................................................ (360) 902-5638
West Virginia ..................................................... (304) 558-7890
Wisconsin .......................................................... (608) 266-8579 (H)
.......................................................................... (414) 521-5063 (S)
Wyoming ........................................................... (307) 777-7786

(H) - Health
(S) - Safety

| Area | Telephone |
|------|-----------|
| Albany, NY | (518) 464-4338 |
| Albuquerque, NM | (505) 248-5302 |
| Allentown, PA | (610) 776-0592 |
| Anchorage, AK | (907) 271-5152 |
| Appleton, WI | (414) 734-4521 |
| Austin, TX | (512) 916-5783 |
| Avenel, NJ | (908) 750-3270 |
| Baltimore, MD | (410) 962-2840 |
| Bangor, ME | (207) 941-8177 |
| Baton Rouge, LA | (504) 389-0474 |
| Bayside, NY | (718) 279-9060 |
| Bellevue, WA | (206) 553-7520 |
| Billings, MT | (406) 247-7494 |
| Birmingham, AL | (205) 731-1534 |
| Bismarck, ND | (701) 250-4521 |
| Boise, ID | (208) 334-1867 |
| Bowmansville, NY | (716) 684-3891 |
| Braintree, MA | (617) 565-6924 |
| Bridgeport, CT | (203) 579-5581 |
| Calumet City, IL | (708) 891-3800 |
| Carson City, NV | (702) 885-6963 |
| Charleston, WV | (304) 347-5937 |
| Cincinnati, OH | (513) 841-4132 |
| Cleveland, OH | (216) 522-3818 |
| Columbia, SC | (803) 765-5904 |
| Columbus, OH | (614) 469-5582 |
| Concord, NH | (603) 225-1629 |
| Corpus Christi, TX | (512) 888-3420 |
| Dallas, TX | (214) 320-2400 |
| Denver, CO | (303) 844-5285 |
| Des Plaines, IL | (847) 803-4800 |
| Des Moines, IA | (515) 284-4794 |
| Englewood, CO | (303) 843-4500 |
| Erie, PA | (814) 833-5758 |
| Fort Lauderdale, FL | (954) 424-0242 |
| Fort Worth, TX | (817) 428-2470 |
| Frankfort, KY | (502) 227-7024 |
| Guaynabo, PR | (787) 277-1560 |
| Harrisburg, PA | (717) 782-3902 |
| Hartford, CT | (860) 240-3152 |
| Hasbrouck Heights, NJ | (201) 288-1700 |
| Honolulu, HI | (808) 541-2685 |
| Houston, TX | (281) 286-0583 |

| | |
|---|---|
| Houston, TX | (281) 591-2438 |
| Indianapolis, IN | (317) 226-7290 |
| Jackson, MS | (601) 965-4606 |
| Jacksonville, FL | (904) 232-2895 |
| Kansas City, MO | (816) 483-9531 |
| Lansing, MI | (517) 377-1892 |
| Little Rock, AR | (501) 324-6291 |
| Lubbock, TX | (806) 472-7681 |
| Madison, WI | (608) 264-5388 |
| Marlton, NJ | (609) 757-5181 |
| Methuen, MA | (617) 565-8110 |
| Milwaukee, WI | (414) 297-3315 |
| Minneapolis, MN | (612) 664-5460 |
| Mobile, AL | (334) 441-6131 |
| Nashville, TN | (615) 781-5423 |
| New York, NY | (212) 466-2482 |
| Norfolk, VA | (757) 441-3820 |
| North Aurora, IL | (630) 896-8700 |
| North Syracuse, NY | (315) 451-0808 |
| Oklahoma City, OK | (405) 231-5351 |
| Omaha, NE | (402) 221-3182 |
| Parsippany, NJ | (201) 263-1003 |
| Peoria, IL | (309) 671-7033 |
| Philadelphia, PA | (215) 597-4955 |
| Phoenix, AZ | (602) 640-2007 |
| Pittsburgh, PA | (412) 395-4903 |
| Portland, OR | (503) 326-2251 |
| Providence, RI | (401) 528-4669 |
| Raleigh, NC | (919) 856-4770 |
| Salt Lake City, UT | (801) 487-0073 |
| Sacramento, CA | (916) 566-7470 |
| San Diego, CA | (619) 557-2909 |
| Savannah, GA | (912) 652-4393 |
| Smyrna, GA | (770) 984-8700 |
| Springfield, MA | (413) 785-0123 |
| St. Louis, MO | (314) 425-4249 |
| Tampa, FL | (813) 626-1177 |
| Tarrytown, NY | (914) 524-7510 |
| Toledo, OH | (419) 259-7542 |
| Tucker, GA | (770) 493-6644 |
| Westbury, NY | (516) 334-3344 |
| Wichita, KS | (316) 269-6644 |
| Wilkes-Barre, PA | (717) 826-6538 |
| Wilmington, DE | (302) 573-6115 |

**Region I**
(CT,* MA, ME, NH, RI, VT*)
JKF Federal Building
Room E-340
Boston, MA  02203
Telephone: (617) 565-9860

**Region II**
(NJ, NY,* PR,* VI*)
201 Varick Street
Room 670
New York, NY 10014
Telephone: (212) 337-2378

**Region III**
**(DC, DE, MD,* PA, VA,* WV)**
Gateway Building, Suite 2100
3535 Market Street
Philadelphia, PA  19104
Telephone: (215) 596-1201

**Region IV**
(AL, FL, GA, KY,* MS, NC,
SC,* TN*)
Atlanta Federal Center
61 Forsyth Street, SW, Room
6T50
Atlanta, GA 30303
Telephone: (404) 562-2300

**Region V**
(IL, IN,* MI,* MN,* OH, WI)
230 South Dearborn Street
Room 3244
Chicago, IL 60604
Telephone: (312) 353-2220

**Region VI**
(AR, LA, NM,* OK, TX)
525 Griffin Street
Room 602
Dallas, TX 75202
Telephone: (214) 767-4731

**Region VII**
(IA,* KS, MO, NE)
City Center Square
1100 Main Street, Suite 800
Kansas City, MO 64105
Telephone:  (816) 426-5861

**Region VIII**
(CO, MT, ND, SD, UT,* WY*)
1999 Broadway, Suite 1690
Denver, CO 80202-5716
Telephone: (303) 844-1600

**Region IX**
(American Samoa, AZ,* CA,*
Guam, HI,* NV,*
Trust Territories of the Pacific)
71 Stevenson Street
Room 420
San Francisco, CA 94105
Telephone: (415) 975-4310

**Region X**
(AK,* ID, OR,* WA*)
1111 Third Avenue
Suite 715
Seattle, WA 98101-3212
Telephone: (206) 553-5930

*These states and territories operate their own OSHA-approved job safety and health programs (Connecticut and New York plans cover public employees only). States with approved programs must have a standard that is identical to, or at least as effective as, the federal standard.

www.ingramcontent.com/pod-product-compliance
Lightning Source LLC
Chambersburg PA
CBHW051827170526
45167CB00005B/2193